Advanced Praise for UNSTUCK YOURSELF

"A book on sales that deals with the reality of how to have a fulfilling career while growing the bottom line. Klyn teaches in a new and refreshing way that engages the entire sales system, not just the individuals and their managers. I bought a copy for everyone on my retail sales team, and we started using these tactics in our daily huddles."

- Doug Carey, EVP West Gate Bank

"Captivating and authentic, Klyn challenges professional salespeople to become top-performing producers by leveraging their mindset. UNSTUCK YOURSELF is a must-read for every growth-focused organization that believes in developing leaders who develop future leaders. Klyn's winning approach helps professional salespeople create new value for their customers."

- Kent Gregoire, CEO, Symphony Advantage, Inc.

"All results are preceded by action. UNSTUCK YOURSELF tackles the biggest sales challenge that virtually all sales professionals face at some point in their career: failure to take consistent action. Klyn brings her experience, passion, and authenticity to life in this action-packed roadmap for sales success. UNSTUCK YOURSELF is a must for

sales teams and sales leaders wanting to push beyond their comfort zone."

- John Ryan MBA, MSW, Master Trainer of NLP

"I have seen wonderful people enter the sales profession only to come to believe they're terrible at everything quickly. Whether it's hearing 'no' over and over again or being put off by that one prospect who could change everything, nobody is immune from the disappointment that comes from trying to sell for a living. In UNSTUCK YOURSELF, *Klyn shows you how to break out from fear, find meaning in your work, and take action necessary to succeed on your terms."*

- Travis Luther, Founder - Queen Anne Pillow Company

"Success does not come by accident. You need a plan. Klyn's 30-day Road map gives you that plan. Execute, and you will fly! Read this book!"

- Todd Toback, Former Fortune 100 Sales Executive/ Real Estate Entrepreneur

"I've had the pleasure of attending Klyn's sales playbook masterclass, and this book elaborates on the mindset of sales success as well as how managers can grow their teams. I bought a copy, read it, gave it out to my team. I'm confident we will see growth."

- Andy Cheng, CEO Masks Guru Inc

"When I first met Klyn at a conference of 500+ where I was keynoting, she immediately stood out. The key was the quantity and quality of life questions she hammered at me. Now, in UNSTUCK YOURSELF, *she asks the questions that every aspiring Top Producer needs to answer. I join Klyn in challenging you to wrestle down the answers- do that, and success is yours!"*

- Jack Daly, Serial Entrepreneur, Best Selling Author, and World Recognized CEO Coach

*"*UNSTUCK YOURSELF *is something I encourage every sales professional to take on. At the Institute for Excellence in Sales, we work with some of the world's top sales leaders to help them acquire, motivate, retain, and elevate top tier talent. This continues to get harder to do as customers continue to control the sales process and global economic and health challenges affect business growth. Sales professionals need all the mental acuity they can attain, and her process makes that happen."*

- Fred Diamond, Founder Institute for Excellence in Sales and Sales Game Changers Podcast and Webcasts

"Klyn Elsbury has overcome every challenge and obstacle that has come her way. Sales reps and seasoned professionals can find every excuse as to why they can't win and succeed, especially when a crisis hits. This is not the case for Klyn. She thrives and overcomes any crises, personally and professionally, and turns them into opportunities. I highly recommend UNSTUCK YOURSELF *to any leader*

guiding a sales team and to those who are looking to make a shift at living their greatest life and having a successful sales career."

- Anya Krebs, CEO Office Space Copier

"In a time when much of the world has gone crazy, and people are overwhelmed, Klyn Elsbury provides simple, concise, and effective tactics for mastering our crucible moments and increasing sales. UNSTUCK YOURSELF is not going to be one more thing added to readers' to-do list. Rather, readers will enjoy Klyn's straight-to-the-point style and easily implementable daily action items."

- Crystal Washington, Technology Strategist, and Futurist

"This should be required learning for every aspiring attorney, sales professional, manager, or business owner! Even those who aren't technically in a 'sales' position will generally have an easier go at life if they can negotiate successfully with others. UNSTUCK YOURSELF is a different approach to success. Klyn gives just enough of the "why" before she pulls you right through her 'how'. And her 'how' is a logical, comprehensive plan to improve your sales—and your life--- in thirty days."

- Ashley Pepitone ESQ, Attorney and Legal Tech Entrepreneur

"The ONLY way top performers deliver consistently is with effective strategies to push through the hard times — the times when others become 'stuck.' In this practical and enlightening book, Klyn Elsbury provides professionals that missing piece between strategy

and execution; intention and action. Klyn gives you both the why and the how-to get 'unstuck.' Read it with a highlighter in your hand and write all over this book!"

- David Avrin, President, The Customer Experience Advantage

"Intelligence is learning from your own mistakes. Earning intelligence is painful. It leaves bruises. It usually isn't fun. On the other hand, wisdom is a generous gift, given with humility by someone willing to share their own experience to save you from the pain of learning on your own. For those looking to be intelligent without bruises, this book offers a generous gift of wisdom."

- Mike Maddock, CEO of Maddock Douglas & Flourish Forums

"Klyn has done it again! This is a must-read for anyone in sales who wants to have a career, not just a job."

- Nikhil Choudhary, CEO Zenith Engineers

"Klyn lays out a 30-day action plan to improve sales performance. At first, I thought this would be another mindset book, but the straight forward, no BS approach, with actual tactics proved to be a game-changer for myself and my team."

- Duran Inci, CEO Optimum 7

"Klyn is a champion saleswoman who somehow makes neuroplasticity understandable and entertaining! UNSTUCK YOURSELF is a practical, relatable guidebook that will help you *jumpstart (or restart!) your career in 30 days by understanding how your brain works. Do yourself a favor and start it today. Then, reread it every 30 days until you can quote it by heart."*

- Brittany Hodak, Entrepreneur & Speaker

"Klyn gets straight to the mind of a top producer while captivating the heart of selling. This book should be required as a 30-day sales training program for every salesperson in your company."

- David Mammano, Host of The Gonzo Experience Podcast

"I'm so passionate about this book and Klyn's training methodology because I've seen firsthand how unlearning everything I knew about sales increased our closing percentage 71%, improved the quality of conversations with our customers, and created lasting motivation in our team."

- Jeff Shelton, CEO of Wholesale Warranties

UNSTUCK YOURSELF

A 30-day proven sales playbook that uses
neuroscience to improve your sales career

Klyn Elsbury

With a special message from Jeff Hoffman,
Global Entrepreneur from
Priceline.com/Booking.com and uBid.com
and
Chairman, Global Entrepreneurship Network

Foreword by Jeff Shelton
Co-Produced by Ric Groeber

MK Foundation

San Diego, CA

UNSTUCK YOURSELF

A 30-day proven sales playbook that uses neuroscience to improve your sales career

First edition

Klyn Elsbury, Author

Ric Groeber, Co-producer

ISBN ebook 978-1-7364552-0-3

ISBN Paperback 978-1-7364552-1-0

The book is printed in the United States of America.

https://www.missklyn.com/

DEDICATION

UNSTUCK YOURSELF is dedicated to all those who want to grow, develop, and lead. It's for my family, the readers & the 60,000 fans who have shared their stories, struggles, and successes with me. You've taught me that champions are built, not born.

Now, get to work.

Instructions for reading

UNSTUCK YOURSELF

I magine a month from now your sales are improving, you've managed to take back control of your mental and emotional health, and you've had quality time with your friends and loved ones. You find yourself experiencing more energy, more motivation, and less stress.

How is this possible? By committing to this 30-day playbook, you can. As you read one chapter a day for 30 days in a row, you will begin to unravel parts of your past that have held you back from peak performance.

Ideally, before you start your day, go through these questions thoroughly. Each chapter will build on the previous chapter. Do not skip ahead.

By the end of this book you will have discovered the part of you that is incredibly motivated, driven, and committed to excellence in every aspect of your life.

I believe in two guiding principles when it comes to living an extraordinary life:

1. Champions are built, not born. Your past and current situation are not your final destination. You can always choose what actions you take, regardless of the circumstances of your life. Your past does not define you.

2. Everything is a sale. Regardless of your job title, you have received everything in your life based on your ability to negotiate. Your income, spouse, family, where you live, and your diet are all impacted by the mental chatter that continually works to convince you of the next actions to take. In this book, we will call that the itty bitty head committee. You will start to pay attention to the committee and what it has caused in your life, and then learn how to change those thoughts into ones of purpose, power, and prosperity.

You got this,
Coach Klyn Elsbury

TABLE OF CONTENTS

FOREWORD:
BY JEFF SHELTON,
CEO of Wholesale Warranties

Having done extensive sales training throughout my career before meeting Klyn, I never thought there was much else out there in the sales world that I had yet to learn. To me, every sales book, training method, and technique blended together. I felt I wasn't learning anything new. Every trainer taught the same thing but put a different title on their methodology.

Klyn's insights were unique and different, based on neuroscience with strong attention to pattern recognition and optimization. She could analyze every conversation our representatives had with our customers. She deciphered our text messages, email conversations, and follow up phone calls. She broke down what was working in easy to understand, bite-sized principles that could be taught to incoming hires and scaled.

Up to that point, what I learned from the sales training community I can best describe as the "what to say" and "when they say this, you say that" type of selling. What Klyn has taught me, and my company is best described as "What goal do you want someone else to obtain that you can be directly responsible for?" She destroyed our need for the hard close. We had to unlearn many things we spent years training on. Only then, I started noticing peculiar things during my call monitoring process.

I noticed that our customers never complimented our sales teams on how good of a salesperson they were anymore. And while that might sound like a step in the wrong direction, it wasn't. Before our new approach, I remembered being so proud to hear our customers congratulate my sales representatives when they would say, "You know you're a great salesperson, but" and then go on to say why they couldn't buy right now.

Our sales team didn't sound like they were trying to "sell," and it came off naturally with our new process. On Klyn's first day consulting for us, she told every salesperson that metaphorically they were fired. Sure, the job stayed the same, but we were no longer going to sound like salespeople or closers. We were expected to become world-class educators. A motto that our team still references.

We were closing more deals, but not in the way I was used to, it was the customers asking our reps how they can get started, and almost all of my best, well-crafted, meticulously thought out scripts were thrown in the trash. Had I failed my team? I have to be candid and say that this was a bit of a blow to my ego to know that my way of doing things for so long was so misguided. Then I realized that maybe I didn't fail, but this was what growth and learning looked like. I spent a lifetime reading sales books, feeling like there was nothing new to learn. When I started embracing her teachings, I tried to cling to my old beliefs because it was what I "knew" and was "comfortable with." Klyn was teaching us less about what to say and more about who to be.

We also stopped talking to our customers about price and throwing benefits at them, hoping they would call us back eager to buy. We learned how to strategically build value throughout the calls, regardless of whether they purchased from us or went with a competitor. We became friends with our customers through education and information, not deep discounts, and relentless pesky follow-ups.

Now we lead customers to the best decision for them, not for our agenda. We taught them the value of human connection, and as a team, we created values around growing, developing, and training each other. Everything was different, and the energy in the office during this year improved. We started having million-dollar months regularly, we enjoyed talking with our customers, and when one teammate struggled, others would step in to build additional training. Hence, nobody was "left behind."

I looked around and noticed that I no longer had a sales team. I had a group of world-class educators. And what I discovered was that instead of training them frequently, they took their own initiative and started teaching me and each other. This allowed the leadership schedules to be freed up and focus on bigger goals than we thought possible without hiring any additional people because we were an efficient machine.

A career in sales isn't about selling. Sales is about learning how to grow, develop, and train everyone you encounter with the will, skill, and desire to implement. Sales is about building champions instead of relying on charisma and hard closes. Whether you are selling an enterprise solution, trying to get hired in a new job, (or in Klyn's case, why a drug company should approve you for a life-saving drug), the quality of your life is dependent on your ability to communicate and influence effectively.

I'm so passionate about this book and her training methodology because I've seen firsthand how unlearning everything I knew about sales increased our closing percentage 71%, improved the quality of conversations with our customers, and created lasting motivation in our team.

- Jeff Shelton, CEO of Wholesale Warranties

A SPECIAL MESSAGE FROM JEFF HOFFMAN,

GLOBAL ENTREPRENEUR FROM PRICELINE.COM/BOOKING.COM AND UBID.COM
AND
CHAIRMAN, GLOBAL ENTREPRENEURSHIP NETWORK

I once read a sign that said, "Everybody wants to be successful, just until they find out what it takes."

Truer words have never been said.

We all have a vision of where we want to be. Where we think we BELONG. A place in the world that's rightfully ours. But the distance between our vision board and our reality often seems infinite.

So what does it take to climb your personal mountain? To achieve the success you have dreamed about for years? Passion? Perseverance? Hard work?

It turns out that it takes all of these things, plus more. So let's take a little walk down the path to success and see what tools and talents we need to make it to the end.

The first tool in our toolbelt is CLARITY. Many people think of success as getting rich. They measure it in money. But not only is being successful about much more than just money, but it's also getting to a specific place in your life, a particular set of circumstances that define a 360 view of your life, not just your bank account.

Clarity helps define a detailed vision of your ultimate goal and serves as your North Star to guide you in good decision making, so the moves you make along the way lead you to the place you want to be. To achieve clarity, write down a description of what your day and your week look like when you achieve success.

They say, "be careful what you wish for," so make sure you wish for what you want. How much money will it take to make you happy? What day-to-day responsibilities will you have? What will your home and family life look like? Friends? How about your physical health? Or spiritual and emotional health? Happiness is a multi-variable equation. The more clarity you define in what you are ultimately seeking, the more likely you will steer yourself in the right direction for success.

In addition to clarity, success takes FOCUS. Sometimes people want to "hedge their bets" by working on many possible paths to success at once, but the truth is that no Olympic athlete ever won a gold medal by practicing six different sports at a time. To win a gold medal in life and business, you need to STOP working on anything directly in line with your path to success. Narrow your focus, simplify your to-do list and stick to doing whatever you do best in the world. Win a gold medal at YOUR sport, not everyone else's.

The third critical skill you need to develop on your path to success is EMPATHY. I knew as a leader that in order for my business to grow, I had to be a good presenter so I could close sales, attract investors, and more. That turned out to be true. But those are TALKING skills, and no one told me how important my LISTENING skills would turn out to be.

Empathy is so much more than just being a good listener. It's the art of genuinely HEARING people and connecting with people. Understanding people. Ultimately my ability to dramatically grow my business and achieve success came from the time I put into strengthening my empathy muscle to understand what the customer wanted to buy, not what I was selling them. And what the investor came to hear, not just what I wanted to say. Empathy also includes learning to ask the right questions so that you listen to what the world is trying to tell you, instead of just the answer to the specific question you asked.

Let's add one more essential requirement for achieving success, to combine with the tools we just strapped around our waist to make sure we are equipped and able to climb to the heights of success we knew we would one day achieve.

That last essential skill is TEAMWORK. I don't think my success started until the day I recognized that I could not do this alone, and neither can you. The actual key to success is to surround yourself with people smarter than you, then get out of their way and let them lead you to victory. So what does that mean to you?

It means you need to spend less time running the business yourself and more time hunting for exceptional people to help do it with you. Or to cultivate and develop the people who are currently on a team with you. Each of us is truly only talented at one major thing – finance, marketing, engineering, etc. So pick yours, and find people better than you in every other functional area. There's an old African proverb that says, "If you want to go fast, go alone. But if you want to go far, go together". Whoever said that probably went very far.

Success is within your reach. You just have to be willing to do what it takes to get there. And what it takes is clarity, focus, empathy, and a team of people smarter than you.

- Jeff Hoffman, Global Entrepreneur from Priceline.com/Booking.com and uBid.com and Chairman of Global Entrepreneurship Network

PREGAME HUDDLE:

The experiences that shape a person's trajectory of life are called crucibles, after the vessels medieval alchemists used in their attempts to turn base metals into gold. A crucible is often a defining moment in someone's life, usually sudden and unplanned.

There are three primary personality responses when there's a crucible event:

1. People who sink lower than they originally were and could not bring themselves back out of it. They think with a victim mentality, blame others, cannot forgive, and exude imposter syndrome. These are the people who have received multiple opportunities for success but claim "it just wasn't the right moment for them."

2. People who go back to their usual way of life and continue as if nothing happened. Usually, we associate these people with

having denial or being unable to face and confront their problems.

3. People who push through adversity and go on to create unfathomable success.

I want to open up with you and share my crucibles, and then dedicate the rest of this book to helping you define and interpret yours. Your life is a culmination of how you interpreted crucible moments. The meaning you give to the events that happen in your life ultimately determines your actions. I want your life to be one of the actions taken that set you uniquely apart from others. I want you to be the next success story.

I was 24 hours old when I experienced my first crucible. My stomach was not working correctly, so I was airlifted to a new hospital. Within a few hours I was diagnosed with cystic fibrosis. I spent the first six months of my life in the neonatal intensive care unit.

Every year of my life I am routinely hospitalized in what is called a "tune-up." A tune-up is a two-week hospital stay where I endure a 24-7 antibiotic IV drip to clear the infections in my lungs. After my fiftieth hospitalization, my veins could no longer support the IVs, and I underwent surgery to get a port-o-cath (which is a device that feeds medications up through my jugular and into my heart).

In 2001 I slipped into a month-long diabetic coma that doctors feared would cause permanent brain damage. Fortunately, my brain is intact, although my pancreas no longer functions. As a diabetic, I now inject insulin up to 4 times a day. I also spend an hour every morning and an hour every evening attached to various nebulizers to open my airways to attempt to help me breathe.

When infections begin, I can go from hiking summits of volcanoes in Costa Rica or 12-mile hikes in Yosemite to coughing up blood and needing oxygen in mere weeks. Any day now an infection could begin again. And my chances of rebounding diminish due to antibiotic resistance.

When I was born the life expectancy was only 14. If you were born today with CF you could expect to live to be 37 years old. I'm almost 33. Simple math says that 89% of my life is over. With 67 hospitalizations in those 32 years, over 50% of my life has been inside hospital walls.

When I was in my mid-twenties, I signed the papers for my life to be handed over to the social security department and joined the millions of people legally classified as disabled. I remember it very clearly.

Until that moment I was in charge of the recruiting processes for a multi-million dollar private healthcare company. My sole responsibility was to call people who were relatively happy in their careers and convince them to leave their stable jobs to join our company. I finally found my life's work, or so I thought.

My sales journey started in kindergarten when I convinced my parents to build a restaurant in their garage. Although we lived in a small town in Iowa, I knew if I had my restaurant, I'd have the money to leave and expand my horizons. I went around the neighborhood and aggressively promoted Klyn's Kitchen, a place where you could have a fresh bowl of cereal for only a quarter before walking to the bus stop.

That was my first attempt at selling, and I made two dollars that month. I started to realize that Klyn's Kitchen was not a significant life goal. Shortly after that realization, the company quickly went bankrupt when my brother found my quarters in my Barbie playhouse and stole them.

From that moment on, I became obsessed with learning how to sell and negotiate. I practiced negotiations with the school nurses, who granted me the ability to take my digestive enzymes at the lunch table instead of going to their office when I needed pills. In middle school, I negotiated with teachers to give me extra time to complete homework to make up for the three months of every school year I was in the hospital. I convinced the principal to host a fundraiser for Cystic Fibrosis awareness, and if I beat our fundraising goal, we will take a pig off the farm and he would kiss it during a pep rally.

While in the hospital, I negotiated with the charge nurse (the leader of the nursing department) to give me the friendliest nurses. I negotiated with the janitors to provide me with extra tokens to use in the vending machines. I negotiated with doctors to release me from the ward a day early, preferably on a Thursday, to have a long weekend with my family before school started.

The pattern continued through middle school and high school. I was always one negotiation away from a dramatically different life. I didn't know what selling meant. I didn't see myself as a salesperson.

I learned about the world of selling at first through my father, who was a territory account representative for a Fortune 500 company. As his career progressed, we were forced to move every year. Besides learning how to interact with different hospital employees, I learned how to build instant rapport with people outside of those walls. We moved so much. In fact, I went to four different high schools.

I did ride alongs with my dad, eavesdropping on sales strategies and techniques while he cold-called prospects and wrote up contracts. I'd come home and learn from my mom, who was negotiating with hospital billing departments and coordinating treatment protocols.

As a young adult, I looked around at the life I was creating and felt a genuine panic set in. I won a sales contest during a college internship for an insurance company. After winning I checked in to the hospital for a 2-week "lung tune-up." I was spending more time those years in hospitals than I was in my dorm room. Unable to balance my failing health with college pressures, I dropped out of school with a 4.0 GPA.

I didn't want to live my remaining days in yet another small town. I packed everything I owned into a beat-up Camaro and moved 1200 miles away from a familiar face, settling in Orlando, Fl. I cold-called companies trying to find employment while I lived in an apartment that I negotiated for $600 a month. I ate ramen. I slept on an air mattress. I had no furniture. All I had was ambition and the rock-solid belief that tomorrow would be better than today.

A month into the process, a financial services firm hired me. Except there was a problem - I hated my career. I found out they offered $1500 recruitment bonuses if you could introduce the hiring department to quality candidates. I would work my shift then go downtown and network to Orlando's young elite. In my spare time, I redid resumes and convinced my new friends to quit their jobs and work for my company. I made more money that year helping the HR department than I did at my actual job.

Soon after, I found out that recruiting was a profession. I walked into the top recruiting company in Orlando and refused to leave until the CEO interviewed me. Not having a degree was a barrier to entry, so I convinced him to hire me under the premise that if I didn't produce results, he should fire me instantly.

Within six weeks, I was a top producer. And then fate stepped in. That year I spent 154 days in the hospital, and we even set up my office to make space for my IV drip and nebulizers. Despite the happiness from my career, the disease was progressing. I knew I wouldn't be able to keep up with it much longer.

Through a series of serendipitous moments, I relocated again to San Diego, California, to be closer to the biotech companies that made drugs to help treat Cystic Fibrosis's progression. By then I worked for a different recruiting company and my lungs were at 30% capacity. I resigned from my corporate sales career one night in the emergency room, believing my time was up. I was devastated. Everything I wanted in my life, including life, was over. I lost my health, house, career, income, and purpose.

The doctors walked out of the room and the night shift nurse walked in. The nasal cannula pumped oxygen through my lungs and I heard her say, "You've had a good run. This is officially end-stage CF. Filing for disability services and government support takes financial stress off you and could help with getting access to medicine." I spent that night alone in the emergency room, listening to the sound of machines beeping. I promised myself that if I ever had a second chance at life I'd make it count. I prayed. I cried. I prayed again. I filed the paperwork and legally handed over my future to government services.

That memory was the beginning of my obsession with what makes people successful and what makes people respond differently to crucibles. I started to wonder what people need to know to achieve success despite the odds? I became obsessed with human potential and the differences between those who succeeded and those who didn't. I noticed the contrast between those with rocks thrown at them who managed to build an empire with the bricks at their feet versus the people buried by the same bricks.

So on my second anniversary of waiting for death, I started writing a book from my hospital bed, beginning to answer those very questions. When it launched, I figured only my mom would read it. I was shocked when *"I AM __ The Untold Story of Success"* hit international bestseller status. My book launch party had over 180 guests! That book has taken me around the country to various stages, keynoting and delivering one-of-a-kind motivational performances on topics of adversity, resilience, and embracing change. I built a company off the success of that book.

With the extra time I had in hospitals, I studied neuroscience, gaining a master's practitioner certification in neurolinguistic programming with an emphasis on hypnotherapy.

If you read the first book, you learned how I went up against pharmaceutical companies to obtain the drug that halted the disease. And if you follow me on social media, you know that it will be over one year since my last hospitalization when this book launches.

I spent the last few years of my life honing my business and programs with selling principles and a neuroscience framework. I dabbled in social media selling for a while, creating a course on building a personal brand and converting online followers into buyers. I felt like I was all over the place, and now in my thirties, I still didn't know who I was. When my now fiance asked me to help train his sales team, admittedly, I didn't think I had what it took. I never had a traditional sales career - who was I to lead them? Who was I to train them? I avoided it because I wasn't sure I could convince myself of my abilities.

Why do I share this with you? With humility, I never saw myself as a salesperson. I never thought my life's purpose was to help others sell. To me, sales were what other people did. I never saw myself as a saleswoman.

You may be newer to sales. You may hate the word sales. Or you may love this profession but question if it is your life calling and purpose. You may not be sure who you are or what your place is in life. You're not alone. Most people spend their lives entirely unsure of who they are or what is possible in their lives.

The first sale you need to make in your career and life is selling your mind that everything is a sale. In life, you don't get what you deserve. You get what you negotiate. Your entire life is a direct result of how well you negotiate.

In sales, you are going to face crucible moments every day. When the moment passes, recognize the only person you need to convince to get back up and try again, despite all obstacles, is yourself. Your mental attitude is the first sale you make with yourself that day. Everything stems from that in the same way everything is a sale. Sales is a head game. Do you want to know what is worse than CF? I mean much, much worse....

Living a long life and not reaching your potential because you don't believe in yourself.

I estimate at the time of this writing, I have hired over 1500 salespeople in my career. I have interviewed thousands of successful CEOs and their management team. I have been blessed to coach and work with top producers in every industry. Implementing these same tactics and mental shifts increased closing percentages by 71% within three months in one company.

This book compiled those experiences and my mental hurdles on how I went from government assistance to a 3x best-selling author, corporate trainer, and keynote speaker within five years. This book will also highlight some of the stories of seemingly miraculous transformations I've seen within people in a relatively short amount of time when you focus on developing leaders and guiding them in accountability.

It starts with you and the desire to win. It begins with your desire to be world-class at what you do and know why you do it. I want you to know you have to be your biggest cheerleader. You have to take the crucible moments in your life and see them as stepping stones to achievement. That's the thing about this profession. Once you see it, you can't "unsee" it. Every part of our life requires negotiation. I have a lot to learn. I always will. And when I feel overwhelmed by the speed of it all and my insecurities, I repeat to myself,

"Champions are built, not born."

DAY 1:

Honesty

"Discipline is the bridge between goals and accomplishment."

- Jim Rohn

No matter where you are in life right now, recognize there's room for improvement. I know that times are often challenging - careers can be stagnant, the economy is unpredictable, and society seems to have lost its way.

And I also know, paradoxically, we live in a time where most significant resources are available to most people. In general, we are safe when we leave our homes. We have a supportive group of friends and family, and the world happens to reward those who work hard to change their current situation rather than let it be the final destination.

You wouldn't have bought this book if you didn't believe that you had what it takes to succeed in your life and sales career. Nor would you have purchased this book if you didn't think you could surpass your goals, raise your expectations, and prove mountains are built from the rocks others have thrown at you.

Before we begin, I want everyone to do a small exercise. Laugh. Do it right now. Sure, it will be fake but give yourself a little chuckle or two quick snorts from your nose. Researchers have found that laughter (even the fake ones) can provide all sorts of benefits, including reducing stress, lowering blood pressure, improving creativity, and releasing healthy endorphins.

The journey ahead might be rough at times so if you find yourself getting overwhelmed, exhausted, or just feel like you are in a rut – stop, take a deep breath, and give yourself a little chuckle. You'll be amazed at how much better that little spark will make you feel.

Now let's get started with the hard work. Go to the closest mirror and look at your reflection. This book will provide you with tough love. Look in that mirror and listen to that gut reaction you have. Where have you been slacking? Are you fit? Are you as healthy as you can be? Are you eating the foods that give your future self energy and stamina? Do you have any habits you need to eliminate? How sharp is your mind and what are you doing to improve neuroplasticity? Do you know what neuroplasticity is?

Make a comprehensive list of what that itty bitty head committee is telling you. Allow yourself to beat yourself up a little bit. You need to.

Your competition can't beat you if you know your weaknesses and work to overcome them.

COACH KLYN'S HOMEWORK TO DO BEFORE DAY 2:

List 4 things you are committed to changing in the next 30 days. That's one a week.

1._____

2. _____

3. _____

4. _____

DAY 2:
Standards

"The way to get started is to quit talking and begin doing."

-Walt Disney

I f you wrote an extensive list on Day 1, then kudos to you. I've hired over 1800 salespeople in my recruiting career and then as a corporate recruiting consultant for various Inc 5000 and Fortune 1000 companies.

I noticed that when you ask a high achiever to look in the mirror and come up with four things they know they need to change, they will create 10. An average performer will write 4-5. And those who aren't genuinely committed to success will write out one or two and then shift to something else that provides short-term gratification.

None of these approaches are wrong, per se. They all serve that individual. Most people do not want to look in the mirror and analyze their faults, so if you did, give yourself some credit. Just don't bask in the glory when there is work to do.

Let me tell you a quick story. One of the call center reps I coached sat in the front row of a training class and took so many notes, I thought they would need surgery on their hand after the 3-hour training.

At the close of the training, I gave everyone homework. I instructed the reps to commit to raising their standards (which we'll get to in Day 3) and strive to increase their outbound prospecting activities by 100 dials in the next month.

She thought she needed to call 100 more prospects that week! And she did. While the other representatives were busy talking, taking breaks, and wasting their time, she figured out ways to accomplish more activity in less time. A bottom of the pack performer, suddenly she was 3rd in the whole company. Why? She developed the habit of raising her standards. You become the air you breathe.

Psychologists call this a *"schedule of reinforcement."* By setting specific goals and reinforcing yourself when you meet them, you are strengthening your intended behavior. This is the same strategy dog trainers use to get their dogs to do all sorts of tricks like sit, speak, and roll-over. And just like training Fido, the changes won't happen overnight. As you keep setting those goals and giving yourself a pat-on-the-back when you reach them, eventually, you will develop habits just like that call center rep did.

COACH KLYN'S HOMEWORK TO DO BEFORE DAY 3:

Out of the four things you are committed to improving in the next 30 days, what can you do to raise your standards in each section?

Example: *"I want to call more prospects this month."* Raised to: *"I will have 30 more productive conversations with potential buyers this month."*

1._____

2. _____

3. _____

4. _____

DAY 3:
Superpowers

"Become the person who would attract the results you seek."

-Jim Cathcart

You have to know what your selling superpower is. If I ask 100 salespeople why I should buy from them, I hear things like:

1. We are the highest rated.

2. Our customer service is the best.

3. We have a great price.

4. We care about our customers.

Listen, I mean no disrespect - those aren't superpowers anymore. Customers expect those things now. I want to know what makes you different. The company and product differentiation are essential, and also, so are you as a representative. I want to know your superpower and why customers will buy from you.

During one of my corporate training programs, I met a sales representative who had the perfect phone voice. When he talks on the phone, it sounds much like what Chet Holmes (late author of The Ultimate Sales Machine) called the late-night DJ voice. It's that soothing jazz voice that melts the prospect into becoming a buyer and enjoying the process of being sold. His superpower was that voice and ability to build instant rapport with anyone. Look for your superpowers and use that to your advantage.

Another example: my superpower is, and has always been, resilience. Surviving 67 hospitalizations from cystic fibrosis, I know a thing or two about adversity and getting through the most challenging and darkest days (which I describe in my first best-seller, _I AM___: The Untold Story of Success_). So in conversations with buyers, I ask about their tough times. I ask about their struggle. I can relate to people who are in the midst of the chaos of their lives and give them hope it gets better.

There's a blend between superpowers and differentiation, that when done correctly, is a game-changer. Let's play a little thought experiment. Jayden wakes up to his cell phone alarm every morning, makes some toast, and reads the news with a cup of coffee. Brianna wakes up to a pre-programmed Alexa inspirational message alarm, makes a banana-kale-V8 smoothie, and just before heading out the door, creates her plan for the day and writes her affirmations in a journal using multi-colored pens and stickers. Between the two, who is more memorable?

Brianna is more unique, fresh, and memorable. Our senses are overloaded with the mundane everyday. Humans are pre-programmed to remember new and fresh experiences. It's the reason why the drive to a new place feels longer than the same commute back home. While you don't need to create detailed, colorful affirmations to stand out, you need to know what makes you, your company, and your product unique and combine it with your superpower.

What is that "thing" that makes you unique? You may have seen it as a disadvantage before. Your adversity is your advantage, and do not listen to anyone who tells you otherwise.

COACH KLYN'S HOMEWORK TO DO BEFORE DAY 4:

Answer these questions:

1. What are the most common compliments you receive from customers?

_____

_____

2. What topic do people ask you for advice on?

_____

_____

3. What common thread has existed throughout all the phases of your life that allowed you to tap into success?

_____

_____

4. If you could teach a class on anything, what would it be? How can you incorporate that as part of your demo's to your prospects?

_____

_____

DAY 4:
Vision

"Everything you've ever wanted is on the other side of fear."

- George Addair

What did you dislike about your last job, company, and product? What did you love about your last job, company, and product?

Chances are, one of these lists was more comfortable for you to write. If you found it easy to list complaints rather than things you loved, it could be problematic.

Psychologists call this the *"negative bias."* Research has shown that adverse events have a more significant impact on our brain than positive ones. You've probably noticed this effect if you've ever let one off-handed comment from a co-worker ruin an entire day that otherwise went well. Another example we've all experienced is when you get in a fight with your significant other and find yourself stewing over all of their annoying habits instead of focusing on the many reasons why you love them.

When you condition your mind to look for the negative and what you don't like, you will continue to find things to support that belief system. It starts innocently enough, for example when you don't get along with your manager. They may micromanage you or the sales process. They may not pay you what you think your value is. These "red flags" exist to keep you from making mistakes in your career or staying in a place that isn't serving you for very long.

Most salespeople focus so much on what they don't want - they forget to focus on what they want. If I ask you, what is it that gets you excited about your company or product? What makes you excited about your industry? If you could wave a magic wand, where would you want to be in 5 years?

The reality is, as a society we are so used to finding what it is we do not want that we have trouble defining our ideal outcomes.

In one company, I was aiding in the hiring process for a potential sales representative with 20 years of experience. He knew how to sell, sell well, and efficiently contribute to any company that hired him.

Unfortunately, there were red flags from the first interview. For example, I asked the candidate to explain what he disliked about each company. He stated, "Getting to the office by a set time is hard for me. I need to make my schedules." For some companies, that's fine. For this company, it's a deal-breaker. They receive a solid list of leads online overnight, and the reps' ability to start dials at 8 am is crucial. This opportunity will never be a fit for a candidate who struggles with coming to work on time.

During the interview process, he discussed how he couldn't trust managers because although he accomplishes his work, they micromanage. What's interesting was the company he was applying for was incredibly progressive. They structure hours for employees based on traffic patterns, have flex hours for top performers, and pay handsomely.

His past baggage ruined his chances because he couldn't focus on what the good was, only what he didn't want. He couldn't see that realistic first-year income after base salary and commission was $100,000 without a college degree!

Don't let your prior baggage, adverse events, and those times when something didn't work out taint your mindset and future possibilities.

Achievers, take some time today and reflect on all that you do want in your profession. Get specific on your perfect day and ideal career. What does it look like?

COACH KLYN'S HOMEWORK TO DO BEFORE DAY 5:

Answer these questions:

1. How is your ideal career structured? What happens in the morning, afternoon, and evening?

    _____

    _____

2. Who (what types of people) do you interact with within the day?

    _____

    _____

3. What kinds of products do you sell? And through what channels?

    _____

    _____

4. What do you want your compensation to be? Is there a base plus commission? Bonus? Do you want a cap?

    _____

    _____

5. Describe your ideal company, career, manager, and team.

    _____

    _____

DAY 5:
Planning

"Your attitude, not your aptitude, will determine your altitude."

-Zig Ziglar

N ow that you know what you want, it's easy to see where there is a misalignment in your life. Are you in a career that isn't working for your ideal lifestyle?

In my corporate workshops, I teach the 5 Steps to Unstuck Yourself. Often, we are too busy working inside our problems. We forget how to disassociate ourselves from the situation and see it for what it really is versus how we feel about it.

1. Know your outcome.

2. Discover your whys/values.

3. Take action.

4. Look for the failures as feedback.

5. Pivot or adapt your action steps while staying focused on the outcome.

If you know your outcome, you need to have a plan on how to achieve it. Many sales representatives never truly defined what they want their success to be like so they are confused about why it hasn't happened.

Do not let that be you. You know your talents, your superpowers, where your performance gap is, and where you must improve. The next few weeks will challenge you to level up even more so. We will go through the rest of this chapter's steps throughout your 30 days, so be prepared. For now, get that calendar. Set aside 2 hours every week to develop your plan.

Do you ever find yourself repeating the same mistakes or bad habits over and over again? For example, do you have a particular part of the house that you know to look at when you accidentally lose your cell phone? Or do you ever think you need something from the grocery store only to come home and find five boxes of it from the other five times you thought you needed it?

We all make mistakes like this. The human brain forms neural pathways every time we repeat a behavior. Over time, these pathways grow stronger and stronger until the action is involuntary. The same mechanism is at play when we make larger decisions such as dating the wrong type of person or pursuing the wrong type of sale. The way to break out of these slumps is to form a plan and execute.

Treat your career as your own business. Teach yourself how to be personally accountable in all situations. Be proactive. You are the CEO of your job. By owning your schedule and calendar in a well-defined plan, you will be ahead of everyone else who becomes preoccupied with mediocrity and wonders why the good things never happen to them.

Good things happen for you when you make them strategically happen.

COACH KLYN'S HOMEWORK TO DO BEFORE DAY 6:

Answer these questions:

1. Where on my calendar can I dedicate 2 hours to strategic planning?

   _____

   _____

2. Book that time on your calendar, recurring every week.

3. What needs to happen every day to achieve my goals? Example: If I want to make $100,000 and I know each sale nets me $1000, I need to know how many calls I need to close to get that $1000, and multiply the difference. **Remember to work your plan backward, writing it down with timeframes and adjustments. From there, build out your daily activities. If you aren't writing your goals down and executing, you're not goal setting.**

   _____

   _____

4. What are the three things I need to eliminate in my life to get back on track? People often stop social media, watch mindless television, and attend seminars/training without implementing what they learned.

   _____

   _____

DAY 6:
Purpose

"You only live once, but if you do it right, once is enough."

– Mae West

H ere's the real sad truth - times are going to be challenging. Customers are going to disappear. Contracts will get canceled. Managers will have bad moods. The economy will collapse. Industries will end.

How the heck are you going to get through that? How do some people achieve significant accomplishments when it seems like nothing is going right? How do some people thrive during the chaos while others crumble?

I speak about this at conferences every year. I like to call it a crucible moment, after the term alchemists in the middle ages gave to the containers that they hoped would turn base metals into gold. A crucible is a sudden life-changing moment, usually unexpected, that shakes a person to the core. It changes everything you thought you knew about life and how to live it.

After years of research on crucible moments, I've discovered one of the things those who go on to achieve greatness have in common is a profound *"why."*

I had just gotten off stage when a territory representative for a pharmaceutical company approached me. I was in a hurry to get back to the airport because of a scheduling mistake, and she offered to drive me.

As we turned out of the parking lot, I noticed a massive purse in the back seat. Now, I don't mean to judge. I have a large bag for my daily medications in the car at all times, allowing me to free up space when I am at a location for a couple of hours. So I asked.

It turns out she has a chronic condition and it was a purse full of medications. I explained why she chooses to work in a harsh industry when legally, she could be qualified as disabled (which I was in the same situation in my twenties).

She is a single mom. She explains that her daughter watches her work every day, and she will work as long as her body allows her because she wants to be a mom of character. She wants her daughter to see how hard-working she is. She leads her family by example, not words.

Every pill she takes, every side effect she experiences, she endures with a happy, healthy mind. She works and maintains her health so her daughter will never look at excuses or difficult times in life and give up.

Her daughter is her motivation to stay healthy in the face of harsh circumstances.

Everyone has somebody watching them. It may be a child, parents, relationship. At some times, it may just be God. Either way, give them a good show every day.

Lean into your why and your purpose. And let it fuel you.

COACH KLYN'S HOMEWORK TO DO BEFORE DAY 7:

Answer these questions, and don't be afraid to dig deep:

1. Who's at stake if you don't grow?

_____

_____

2. Who is watching you and learning from your actions?

_____

_____

3. What happened in your past that shaped who you are?

_____

_____

4. Why does any of this matter to you?

_____

_____

DAY 7:
Action

"Winning isn't everything, but wanting to win is."

- Vince Lombardi

erhaps the worst part of my career is knowing my tactics and techniques can truly help others live a happier, healthier, more motivated life and knowing many people won't take action.

Humans crave knowledge. Our natural curiosity is one of the critical traits that led us out of Africa in our eventual quest to conquer the world. Many times this curiosity derives from an information gap. We know we are missing something in our lives and feel the need to fix it. But sometimes we get addicted to this pursuit and forget to take action. Learning and implementing are two separate events, and we need to treat growth as a two-step process.

Meet Ryan (changed name to protect the guilty). Ryan is a sales representative who does almost all of the right things. He reads sales books by Grant Cardone, Jeb Blount, Jordan Belfort, Jeffrey Gitomer. Ryan attends learning seminars every quarter. He's even paid his commission checks to attend Tony Robbins' business programs.

There's always something he is learning from and taking notes on. As soon as it's over, he's on the prowl for the next one. One day, I channeled my bravery and asked this type A alpha male why he studies so hard.

"I keep looking for something that will work, I can't find it," he shares.

"And what all have you implemented?" I asked. I knew I hit gold when he didn't have an answer to that. I challenged him to spend a Sunday afternoon with a cold drink in his hand and comb-over his years of notes. His notes came from books, newsletters, seminars, podcasts, conferences, and training.

You see, you can have all the heart and knowledge in your field, but if you don't take action, you can't succeed.

Then I asked him to create his perfect picture in his mind of the kind of life he wanted to live and the career he wanted to have. He agreed not to take on any more information until he implements what he's already learned en route to that ideal outcome.

I don't think I need to tell you how his pipeline was full within a few weeks. On top of that, he was happier, less overwhelmed, and more profitable. Two birds.

Remember, some of the greatest top producers of our time have come from unimaginably difficult childhoods. Many who have had privileged lives did not turn out the way they were expected to. Take actions towards achievement, regardless of if someone expects you to succeed.

COACH KLYN'S HOMEWORK TO DO BEFORE DAY 8:

Answer these questions.

1. Create a giant list of what books you've read, listened to, or downloaded.

   _____

   _____

2. Create a list of seminars you've attended, tactical podcasts you've listened to, newsletters you've subscribed to, and online courses you've completed.

   _____

   _____

3. Look at your ideal outcome, as described earlier. What are things you can IMPLEMENT and take ACTION on TODAY and the rest of the month to get you closer to that outcome?

   _____

   _____

4. Put those actions on your calendar and get to it. Eliminate any other "extra" learning until you've implemented what you already know.

DAY 8:
Flexibility

"You just can't beat the person who never gives up."

-Babe Ruth

Failure happens. Trust when it happens, your competition gives up, and you can dig in. Examples can include:

1. Clients are not returning your calls.

2. Customers are canceling their orders.

3. Your family is upset with how little time you have for them.

4. Your boss puts you on a performance improvement plan.

5. You are gaining weight or eating poorly. You haven't worked out in three days.

Failure is the golden ticket. Your current sales trainer has probably explained that a "no" isn't necessarily a "no" from a buyer. A "no" is an objection designed to coax you to explain more or to come up with a solution that meets their needs. It's not an end. It's just part of the process.

It's the same with failure. When things aren't going the way you want, listen to what the underlying cause is. It's always a symptom of something more profound. And when you hear those symptoms, you strike gold!

Have you ever found yourself pursuing a goal long after you've realized that it's not working? This phenomenon is called the *"Sunk Cost Fallacy."* If you have ever forced yourself to go to an event just because you bought a $25 ticket, or choked down an awful dinner because you spent an hour cooking it, then you've been there. The Sunk Cost Fallacy happens because we all have a desire to see our investments succeed. The more money, time, or resources we throw at a problem, the more we want to see it pay off. However, this inclination can cause us to linger on failed endeavors way longer than we should and waste our time and energy going down dead-end paths. As hard as it is to admit, the best thing you can do when you're in this situation is to stop doing it and lean into another solution.

Early in my speaking business, I applied to over 250+ TED Talks. I thought to myself, if I could just get on TED, I'd know I "made it." Then one day, I realized it wasn't the medium for me. The goal was to speak with sales teams. How much time was I spending chasing something that may not make sense? I listened to that failure. It was time to pivot.

Shortly after that realization, I spent my time building relationships with decision-makers rather than blindly applying to an opportunity online. Within weeks I got an offer to speak about life with cystic fibrosis and how lessons of living in hospitals can apply to business. Ultimately, my failures with applications lead me to write a completely different presentation.

The result? I was the highest-rated keynote performer in that organization's history. I was signed by an agent later that year, and my friends, that is why this book is in your hands. I failed my way to being a keynote speaker and applying the lessons I learned along the way to growing a business.

Sometimes God ignores what you think you want and gives you what you need. You just need to be prepared for that moment.

Failure is a gift. When it happens, find a way to reward yourself for recognizing how you've grown and the lessons you've learned.

COACH KLYN'S HOMEWORK TO DO BEFORE DAY 9:

Answer these questions.

1. Where have you failed in the past?

_____

_____

2. How has that failure rerouted you to what success means to you now?

_____

_____

3. What lessons are you learning from your failures?

_____

_____

DAY 9:
Pivoting

"Learn the rules like a pro, so you can break them like an artist."

-Pablo Picasso

You are not a tree. You can move. Hear me - I don't want you to sit in mediocrity because you tried something and it didn't work out. Remind yourself of the end goal, the outcome you want, and then get back to work.

We all fail from time to time. When we do, admitting it to ourselves can be the hardest part. Everyone likes to believe we are right, which is why being wrong can cause so much stress. Psychologists call this *"cognitive dissonance."* It's the phenomenon we experience when we are forced to hold two contradictory opinions, beliefs, or interests. Sometimes we rectify this dissonance by passively admitting defeat and moving on. For example, we could say, "Sorry I was late, but traffic was horrible," when really we know we didn't leave early enough to make it on time. In extreme cases, some people refuse to confront the dissonance by lying to themselves and others, which creates even more stress and dissonance as the lies and half-truths pile up on one another.

Regardless of how we resolve our defeats, the critical part is how we move on from them. I detail this in my first book; I *AM___: The Untold Story of Success*. It's so hard to open up about how we aren't perfect, how we mess up, and how we embarrass ourselves in the process. Publishing that book took every ounce of courage I had because it was the first time I bared my soul to my followers. There was a risk that it wouldn't work out, that nobody would buy it, that I would be faced to confront my inadequacies.

I decided to move forward and publish because I realized when things aren't going right for you, you have an opportunity to pivot. Look at what opportunities lie ahead and what that can mean for you and your "why." Then get back to the drawing boards and rewrite your plan while keeping the goal in mind. If the book failed, I would take that as a sign to press forward in another area of my life. You'll hear countless trainers tell you that the key is to fail fast. At the very least, your failures will show you the direction you need to take so you can pivot.

Failure is a great thing. It takes out the competition. It destroys the psyche of those who have big dreams but little self-worth. Failing is never a result - it is merely a mechanism designed to teach you how to pivot and change. Analyze failure as a way to find the ultimate success formula.

COACH KLYN'S HOMEWORK TO DO BEFORE DAY 10:

Answer these questions.

1. Where in your life do you feel you have failed?

   _____

   _____

2. What lessons came from that experience?

   _____

   _____

3. Has there ever been anyone who got through a similar failure and succeeded?

   _____

   _____

4. How can you pivot and remain flexible while staying true to your ideal outcome?

   _____

   _____

DAY 10:
Model the Masters

"High expectations are the key to everything."

-Sam Walton

Failure doesn't have to be the only way we grow. A great way to short-cut the learning process is to emulate others who are doing things right. This is called *"observational learning,"* and it is built into each of us from birth. Researchers Andrew N. Meltzoff and M. Keith Moore observed infants as young as 42 minutes old imitating their parents when they opened their mouth and stuck out their tongue! Why go through the pain of trying, failing, and trying again when the right answer can be a google search, book, or interview away?

It was my first day as a healthcare recruiter in Orlando, Florida. I had no degree. I had no skills. I had no income. Walking into the call center, I felt beads of sweat drip down my neck. My boss put me in a cubicle next to the top representative of the company.

Nervous, I tried to strike up a conversation. She looked at me and said, "Hey, new girl, I'm here to make money. I have a full day. You can listen to me and take notes, but most don't survive in this job. I'm not here for a small chat." She looked back at her computer, pulled a file, and got to work.

She was a master. The phone would only be put down long enough for her left hand to punch in the next digits for the next call. And while it was ringing or while she was leaving a voicemail, she finished notating the last call in the CRM. It was a carefully orchestrated dance she did between prospects, noting the database, calling the next candidate, and closing.

How many times are you working only to fill the gaps of time with a small chat or the excuse you need to notate a system? The average call rings four times before sending it to voicemail. The average voicemail is 15-30 seconds long. That's a good 45 seconds between calls where you can finish your notes.

Look to the masters in your industry. See what it is they are doing differently. Offer to buy them lunch or shadow them. I would advise you not to ask questions but to watch. If you asked her what she did to hit $150,000 a year in a call center, she wouldn't have known how to explain it. You watch her and take notes. You see what the differences are. Pay to shadow them if you must.

Did you read the special message from Jeff Hoffman, Philanthropist and founder of Priceline.com, at the beginning of this book? If not, then go check it out now. The ROI is more than you can fathom.

COACH KLYN'S HOMEWORK TO DO BEFORE DAY 11:
Answer these questions.

1. Identify the high achievers in your industry and company.

   _____

   _____

2. Ask them if you can shadow them for a day. (When I did this, I didn't talk to them. Instead, I just watched and noticed what they did. If you tell them it won't disrupt their day, you won't make small talk, and you will get them lunch, then they most likely won't say "no.")

3. Identify what the differences are between your day and theirs.

   _____

   _____

4. Create a plan for how you will implement those differences.

   _____

   _____

5. Implement those differences.

DAY 11:
"Can" Your Plan

"Prior proper planning prevents piss poor performance"

- Unknown and also my dad

Before you get on the call with your prospect, create a mental checklist to ensure you are prepared. "Am I prepared?" I'm not talking about the pen, paper, presentation, stats, charts, etc.... You must be readily prepared to answer whatever comment or objection the client might throw at you. Top producers know what to say in every part of the sales cycle because they plan for the potential responses.

I was in Nashville with my fiance after an event, and we decided to unwind by listening to live music at one of the country bars. I love live music. I cry, laugh, relate to the artists, and always learn something new. The singer asked for song requests from the audience. Unfortunately, one of the requested songs she had never heard before. Recognizing this is an opportunity, she decided to try it anyway and announced it was a new attempt. As she started to belt out the tune, her voice scratched, and it was an immediate failure.

A guy in the audience yells, "Come on, honey, try it again!" It occurred to me, I wouldn't know what to do if I had messed up like that in front of a crowded bar.

What does she do? She's a pro. So she laughed at herself and commented into the mic, "Baby, I thought I told you to stay in the truck? Ladies and gentlemen, meet my now EX-husband."

Brilliant! She had a canned response for when that would happen but shared it in a new and refreshing way that the audience hadn't heard. The top representatives at every company know what part of the sales process they are in and have a flow of what to say. I'm genuinely afraid of the representative who "wings" it every time. Some people are blessed with the gift of gab. They can usually come up with great zingers on the fly. But formulating new responses to every situation takes mental fortitude. What will you fall back on when it doesn't work or are having an off day? If you are a hiring manager in an interview with a salesperson and they don't know what to say for any possible objection you throw at them, do not hire them. If they tell you they have their style, run from them. You can't produce consistent results in an inconsistent conversation.

If your customers are giving you an objection, do you know what to say for each one? Do you have a sales playbook that allows you to ask a few questions in the rapport-building stage and then a brilliant transition to get to the next phase? Top producers have a sales playbook and use it during their calls.

COACH KLYN'S HOMEWORK TO DO BEFORE DAY 12:

Answer these questions.

1. Do you find that you have a similar conversation on every call?

   _____

2. Can you change up the tonality, voice, and vibe to feel fresher?

   _____

3. Can you present and educate your customers after the information-seeking phase in a way that entertains and educates AND expresses all of the information in a concise way?

   _____

4. Do you know what to say for every objection raised?

   _____

5. How often do you feel "stumped" on a call? Can you identify all the potential confusing remarks and know what to say for each?

   _____

   Coaches Tip: My company, MK Foundation, specializes in building custom sales playbooks for organizations that are simple and easy to implement and backed by neuroscience. Should you want to learn more about this, email klyn@missklyn.com.

DAY 12:
Momentum

One of the challenges businesses are facing now is shifting to a remote workforce. Companies without stable tracking and the ability to know what their sales teams are up to are scrambling. If the industry is improving and yet a company's sales aren't growing at the same rate - it's a good sign that the workforce isn't being kept accountable.

Your job, as a top performer, is to capitalize on the momentum. When you get a sale, pat yourself on the back and force yourself to immediately contact another prospect. Momentum is your friend. Momentum is the gift you can give yourself.

I've seen so many salespeople who get a big sale then take that day off. You should celebrate your accomplishments and recognize that moment. Winning is infectious. Others can tell when you are great at what you do. People want to be around other winners. People want to be around those who win. Neurons that wire together, fire together.

You can hear a winner when they contact you. You can also hear desperation. Think of the last telemarketer who called you. You could somehow tell they were on the 32nd call of the day. The energy in their voice was gone. They were just spitting out information. You probably hung up on them.

My friend, please don't be the type of salesperson others try to get off the phone!

Alternatively, think back to the last salesperson who you just "knew" right away you'd buy from them or refer others to them. They had energy, stamina, and a winning personality.

Researchers from McGill University studied how fast our brains can perceive confident speech. For their experiment, they had subjects listen to actors say various phrases in three ways; confidently, close-to-confidently, and unconfidently. What they found was astonishing. In as little as 200ms (0.2s), their subject's brains were showing increased activity when listening to confidant speech versus unconfident speech. That's shorter than the time it takes to "Hi! How are you doing today?" and long before you can make any meaningful pitch. Capitalizing on that winning momentum is critical.

Allow yourself to feel victorious at the moment without losing momentum. Don't take the day off after a big sale. Don't run errands that afternoon. Work when you said you were going to work and celebrate off-hours. Your manager sees it. And remember, if you're not out selling, your competition is.

COACH KLYN'S HOMEWORK TO DO BEFORE DAY 13:

Answer these questions.

1. How can you celebrate your next big sale without losing momentum?

_____

_____

2. What is your new process for leveraging momentum?

_____

_____

Side note: If you feel underappreciated and have raised this concern to management, only to find they didn't fix it, reach out to me.

DAY 13:
Rate Yourself

"Refuse to attach a negative meaning to the word 'no.' View it as feedback. 'No' tells you to change your approach, create more value or try again later."

– Anthony Iannarino

Winners know what to do. They create a plan. They work on the plan. They seek out advice and feedback. Top producers know success is built from individual effort while contributing to the greater good of the organization. Your team is watching you. Your peers are watching you. Your manager is always on the lookout for whom they can promote, give more responsibility to, and who will thrive. It may not seem like they are paying attention. They are.

Executives in your company design forecasting and quotas to be just out of reach in hopes that some will create greatness, and others will falter. Most times, they divvy up in meetings representatives into categories of 3. The bottom 3rd are those who they will be trying to get out of the organization. The middle 3rd are people that positively influence culture, create some wins, and minimally contribute to the organization. Lastly, the top 3rd are the overachievers.

Overachievers contribute to an overall culture, create phenomenal results, and are even open to explaining their methods to help them grow. If your company had to divide up the salesforce into thirds today, where would you fit? If you're in the bottom third, you have some work to do. If you're in the middle, you have some work to do. If you're at the top, go back and read the section on momentum.

COACH KLYN'S HOMEWORK TO DO BEFORE DAY 14:

Answer these questions.

1. Are you contributing positively to the corporate culture? How?

_____

_____

2. Where do you rank as far as productivity in your group?

_____

_____

3. Where do you rank as far as profitability in your group?

_____

_____

4. How can you raise the bar for yourself to stay consistently at the top?

_____

_____

_____

_____

DAY 14:
Excuses

"It's not about having the right opportunities. It's about handling the opportunities right."

-Mark Hunter

Friends, this is a tricky one and hard to talk about in our culture. We've all been through some things in our life that aren't fair. Every.single.one.of.us. In the grand scheme of things, our story doesn't matter. It's what we do with it.

Respect the past, but move forward. If your past is terrible, why would you spend your precious time even focusing on it? Stay focused on the prize and the future.

I want you to think about the excuses you've been making in your life, the childhood trauma, the unfair advantages, the people who lied to you or didn't believe in you, the boss who said you didn't have what it takes to succeed in this profession.

Today, that story you've been telling yourself must end.

We are all holding onto something painful from our past. The reality is, it doesn't have to define our current state. The previous situation does not have to determine the final destination.

I want to challenge you to dig deep internally today. Go to a quiet place. Remember the names and see the faces of people who let you down. Think of when you are judged unfairly. Allow yourself time to reflect on hurtful comments from those you knew, liked, and trusted.

Write them down.

Burn that sheet of paper (or if you're in a high fire zone, tear it into a billion pieces).

Ask yourself, what's at stake if you can't overcome these past traumas? Who suffers because you are clinging to these outdated stories of your worth?

Can I be real with you? I've talked a good game the last 15 days, sharing a bit about who I am and my struggles. I dropped out of college. I was fired countless times. I've endured 67 hospitalizations, some as long as six months. I remember so many times that people told me I would never make it in the speaking industry. Fearful they were right, I hired a coach. Even my coach told me not to enter the speaking and corporate training market because my health would deteriorate.

Ironically, that was her story. She attempted to create a training and consulting company to file bankruptcy three years later when she had a health scare. She projected onto me what she truly believed would be my story, based on her own experience.

As you grow, people will project onto you what they are capable of, not what you are. If someone says something that hurts you or is unfair, let it go. Do not listen to it. You're a different person with unique skills and different goals. You wouldn't be reading this today if you didn't genuinely want to succeed at sales.

Let it go.

COACH KLYN'S HOMEWORK TO DO BEFORE DAY 15:

Think of all the people who have attempted to offer you advice that you know wasn't accurate.

1. When was a specific time someone gave you bad feedback?

_____

_____

2. What lessons did you learn? What changes have you since made?

_____

_____

3. How has making those changes impacted your current situation?

_____

_____

DAY 15:
Limiting Beliefs
Aren't What You Think

"Most of the important things in the world have been accomplished by people who had kept on trying when there seemed to be no hope at all."

– Dale Carnegie

What story are you telling yourself? Confidence wins every time. Expect to win. If you expect to lose, you will. If you expect to win, you will. It's your choice.

You've now begun to remember the hurtful experiences you had as a child, the times somebody judged you, the first time a teacher or boss challenged you unfairly, and when your heart was last broken. Think of all the struggles you've had to endure, the times you cried yourself to sleep, or felt a wave of anger so strongly you lost your temper.

Allow yourself to think of how this has impacted your career. How did these experiences shape your family today?

What have these experiences held you back from accomplishing? Is there anything these experiences have prevented you from trying?

Take this short exercise seriously. Go back and let your mind wander. Sleep on it.

At some point in your life, you were taught the list you generated is an example of the limiting beliefs you have.

It isn't. Many people do not fully understand what a limiting belief is.

A limiting belief is something you swear to be true. It's a nonnegotiable truth to how you perceive the world around you. For example, "The sun rises every morning" is an example of a limiting belief. In your eyes, you believe 100% of the time that the sun will rise. Based on your faith, the sun will rise; you make individual decisions for your future. Some of these choices include working out, continuing education, practicing self-care, setting goals, and deepening relationships. Your actions are the result of your belief that the sun will rise tomorrow.

See if you can relate to this example:

Salesperson: "Klyn, I can't make a quota. I am always great at the beginning of the month and lose momentum at the end of the month."

Me: "And after the meditation, did you think of some of the tough life experiences you've had?"

Salesperson: "I was reminded of how we grew up in a low-income family in the midwest, we didn't have much money, and I think that gave me the drive to be successful. However, we got paid the first of the month through social services, and then by the end of the month, we were hungry."

Me: "Can you see how that has affected your attitude and belief system? You close at the beginning of the month, high income, and then at the end, and it's back to famine?"

Salesperson: "Checkmate."

We've all heard that term before, yet so many experts are wrong about what a limiting belief is.

For a moment, think of your brain as a series of parts. Real quick: think of a goal you have unrelated to your career. Let's say you want to run a 10k this year, and you know you haven't done much physically the past month.

Part of you wants to run; part of you wants to stay on the couch.

It isn't a limiting belief. It's a "part."

The salesperson in the above example didn't have a limiting belief. He openly admitted his motivation and ambitions manifested as a young boy.

You can CHOOSE your "part." What "part" do you listen to when the alarm goes off at 6:30 am? The part of you that put your workout shoes by your bed? Or do you listen to the part that hits the snooze button?

Does our salesperson recognize now part of him wants to succeed, and part of him isn't comfortable with a steady stream of success? When faced with self-sabotage in the middle of the month, I instructed him to focus on the part of him that wants to be successful. Focus on the voice in his head that maintains ambition in life and wants to break through perceived barriers from how he grew up.

How do you believe it worked out for him?

You are given the gift by buying this book to listen to the part of you that wants to succeed. When imposter syndrome or guilt about your success, or poverty mindset hits you - listen to the part of your psyche that encourages your success.

COACH KLYN'S HOMEWORK TO DO BEFORE DAY 16:

1. What are some of your "parts"?

_____

_____

2. Write one paragraph about the part of you that believes in worthiness, accomplishment, success, and abundance. When does that part show itself the most? How can you bring that part out more often?

_____

_____

_____

_____

_____

_____

_____

_____

3. Put that paragraph somewhere you see it every day. Remind yourself of the part of you who knows you have what it takes to break the chains that have held you back before

DAY 16:
Strength

"Courage is not having the strength to go on; it is going on when you don't have the strength."

- Teddy Roosevelt

S ales is a head game. Sales is about expecting rejection while staying optimistic. Stand strong. You've been on this challenge for 16 days. You've learned how your mind works and what belief structures have held you back. You've opened your mind to the idea that success is possible and learned how to model those who achieve the things you want to achieve.

Stand strong.

Stay in your lane.

Self-sabotage is a real thing. One of the salespeople I worked with at a biotech company had a habit of changing industries every 18 months. He couldn't own his lane. Any salesperson's goal is to be an expert in their field first, an expert in their company second, and an expert in their geography last. Now that you know what you want, do you have what it takes to stand firm when the shiny object syndrome happens?

I didn't. I bounced around my career so many times, and I'm embarrassed by it. I didn't know who I was or what I wanted out of my life. I can write so passionately because I made all the mistakes I am hoping you don't. The key is to proactively identify what shiny objects will derail you. For me, it was volunteer work. I went so far into volunteer work that I forgot my core business was motivating, inspiring, and developing salespeople. It took me off my path for years. Knowing now what I didn't know then, I would have created a system that allowed me to volunteer without becoming my core focus.

If this has happened to you too, then don't worry. In 2019 the bureau of labor and statistics (BLS) found that the average American had over 12 jobs in their career. Not only that, but job changes were more likely in the beginning and middle of a person's career than the end. Most people struggle to find their focus. The key is to be intentional. Find your focus and work on becoming that expert. What is your potential biggest distraction?

COACH KLYN'S HOMEWORK TO DO BEFORE DAY 17:

1. What shiny objects will cause you to switch lanes?

    _____

    _____

2. Create a list reminding you of the end goal and why it matters.

    _____

    _____

    _____

    _____

    _____

    _____

DAY 17:
Rapport

"Establishing trust is better than any sales technique."

– Mike Puglia

Depending on your industry, there are an estimated 6 to 13 steps to opening a conversation with a buyer and closing the sale. Do you know what those steps are for your industry? Can you run through the list with ease?

Where are you the least knowledgeable?

We teach our 8-step system in my Proactive Pipeline corporate training:

1. Planning

2. Asking questions

3. Educating

4. Custom solutions

5. Objection conversations

6. Closing

7. Servicing

8. Referral mining

The reason I don't have "rapport" here is that rapport isn't a process. It's a byproduct of what happens when a friendly, knowledgeable, well-planned representative has a conversation with a buyer.

Everything in our life is a sale. Life isn't what happens to you. It's what you negotiated throughout your day. For example, convincing my fiance to get a 3-pound dog (he's never had an animal) was a sale. When I convinced pharmaceutical companies to work with insurance so my health could stabilize, I was making a sale. Every part of your life is a sale.

Many of us spend so long building rapport with customers we forget that we need to complete the entire process. Salespeople who enter the profession because they have the "gift of gab" will soon find themselves out of work. In today's marketplace, time is a commodity. Use it with intention and use it wisely.

The best salespeople care about what you struggle with and how you two can find a solution. They build stories into the sales call with relevant, valuable information, and the knowledge and willingness to improve the quality of life is the rapport. Run far and run fast from the trainers who tell you to build rapport for an allocated amount of time at the beginning of the call. Nowadays, buyers are knowledgeable and want information quickly from a competent salesperson. Wasting their time for three minutes, asking about where they live and what they like to do with their families on the weekend is no longer a recipe for success.

In 2006, Harvard Business School's Michael E. Porter and Nitin Nohria conducted a study tracking how 27 executives in various industries spent their time. They discovered that the CEO's they observed worked an average of 62.5 hours per week. Even more eye-opening was how their time was distributed. On average, they logged hours on 79% of their weekend days and 70% of their vacation days, averaging 2.4 hours daily.

Through interviews, they discovered why the grueling schedule was warranted. The CEOs needed to spend time with each constituency in their organization to provide direction, create alignment, win support, and gather the necessary information to make the right decisions. Most of them said they set strict limits on their work to preserve their health and relationships and avoid becoming like race car drivers and treating home like a pit stop.

Your client's time is valuable. They are looking for solutions to their problems, not more work friends. Authentic rapport is the result of asking strategic questions to your buyer throughout the entire conversation.

COACH KLYN'S HOMEWORK TO DO BEFORE DAY 18:

1. Listen to your last ten calls. How many minutes are you spending on just rapport?

   _____

2. How can you build rapport into every section of your process rather than create a dedicated time?

   _____

   _____

   _____

   _____

DAY 18:
Process

"Knowing is not enough; we must apply. Wishing
is not enough; we must do."

-Johann Wolfgang Von Goethe

How many of you read the last section only to realize you may not know your entire sales process? Most companies are so preoccupied with tracking activities in Salesforce or another CRM that they miss the point of why those data points even exist. Tracking was created to inspect what a manager expects. You can spend your entire day tracking your actions, or you can make revenue when you sell.

Hope is not a strategy when it comes to selling. Champions are built, not born. We need to analyze what your sales system is and work it! Ask your sales trainer to identify step by step the processes you need to take. If they don't have scripted responses for each section, ask them to analyze the high performers' calls in your company and build it out.

Your income will improve if you can listen to what the high achievers are doing and duplicate it. Bonus if you help the company grow in the process. Remember the strategy management has for chopping employees into thirds? Any salesperson who is in the first quadrant becomes indispensable. Your time will come.

Remember to keep in mind that you should adjust your sales pitch to the customer's level, not yours. For example, CEOs want to hear about innovative ideas and policies. Accountants want to listen to the numbers. Operations managers wish to listen to details and how your product fits their current system. Middle-managers want to know that your product will bring more security to their careers and improve the company's monetary gain. Always speak to your audience, not to your personal preference.

COACH KLYN'S HOMEWORK TO DO BEFORE DAY 19:

1. What is your step-by-step sales process?

_____

_____

_____

_____

_____

2. Design a script for each step of the sales process. (P.s. you can use a tool like Prezzi to mind-map it out!)

_____

_____

_____

_____

_____

_____

_____

DAY 19:
Secret to Ending Burnout

"You are never too old to set another goal or to dream a new dream."

-C.S. Lewis

Waiting until you have a paycheck to care about your product, industry, company, or productivity is a loser's mentality. Personal accountability will do more for your career than any other tool, tech, or teaching.

Nobody will ever care about your success more than you do. Never wait for tomorrow if you can make it happen today. Build your momentum, processes, and the confidence will follow. The harvest comes after the seed is planted and nourished.

For years, you may struggle not knowing how you will provide for your family. You may question yourself and your place on this planet. The money doesn't always flow immediately. If you find you are in this phase of life, recognize the desire you have to grow is a positive thing. Work your system and process, be aware of the feedback you receive, and implement the changes you need to make. The income will increase. Opportunities arise when you prepare for them. Your entire life can change in a moment if you prepare for that moment.

The secret to ending burnout is to always put opportunities in front of you. I like to think of this principle as being "at the cause." How many times in your day can you cause the rest of your day to unfold?

Kevin is an account executive I've coached. When I analyzed how he worked, I noticed his day was reactive. He focused on putting out fires rather than causing them. His career was stagnant, the pipeline was low, and leads were slow. There were so many things he had to respond to. He couldn't create the momentum for himself.

I advised him to dedicate two hours every morning, 9-11 AM, for doing the kinds of activities that could bring him revenue. He implemented an email strategy, built-out his Linkedin conversations, set up appointments in his CRM, and set the goal of speaking with three new prospects every morning. For the rest of his day, he dedicated himself to being reactive to the day and putting out "fires."

Within a few months, the fires he thought were urgent and vital faded away. The truth is, very few things that seem urgent are critical. He delegated most of his activities to other team members. His manager saw his sales improve and incentivized him further by hiring him an assistant. He was no longer a paper pusher but back into selling mode.

The secret to Kevin's success can be found in his ability to tap into a better part of his brain. As Daniel Kahneman, author of the best-selling book *"Thinking fast and slow"* points out, our brain operates in two modes. System 1 is fast, instinctual, and emotional, while System 2 is slower, more deliberate, and logical. Our Systems 1 brain is excellent at solving immediate problems to get through the day, but system 2 can create new ideas and better opportunities. When Kevin gave his System 1 brain a rest and allowed his System 2 brain to work, he unleashed a powerful tool that was with him all along.

Of course, he took on this experiment when he made very little from his day-to-day efforts. You can't improve your income if you can't cause more revenue to flow. Focus on the growth process and being proactive, the results will happen. Income will improve.

When you feel yourself getting defeated, focus on creating revenue.

COACH KLYN'S HOMEWORK TO DO BEFORE DAY 20:

1. What activities do you do that lead to more sales?

_____

_____

_____

_____

2. How often are you doing them?

_____

_____

_____

_____

3. How can you do them more effectively?

_____

_____

_____

_____

DAY 20:
Socials

"Whatever you are, be a good one."

-Abraham Lincoln

R eal professionals are in control of the thoughts and content they post to social media.

Rachel (changed name to protect the guilty) is a mid-twenties female with a growing business. A quick scroll online, you'll discover Rachel is quite the extremist. There is nothing wrong with stating your beliefs and opinions, especially when creating progressive and systemic change in the world. Go for it.

However, watch what you are posting in the comments section on your social media feeds. Be considerate when others disagree with you. Your customers, colleagues, bosses, and future are all googling you now.

It's easy. Did you know that as of September 2020, if I save your name on my phone, Instagram alerts me to your account via phone number?

If you post something controversial and then attack those who disagree, you're in for a challenging career. It takes four seconds for that contact you've been praying for to unfollow or delete you.

Rachel was hoping to secure a deal with an investor in her startup. It was a great product and she believed in it so strongly. She even took out a second mortgage to fund it until she could find an investor.

She streamlined every part of her business. She dreamed of the day she could run a large company and team. On the surface, her business continued to flourish.

Unfortunately, Rachel didn't realize people visited her social media and forgot to consider how she treated others who had differing opinions than hers. She frequently posted controversial thoughts. When someone disagreed with her, she attacked them in the comments section. Her condescending comments were out for everyone to see, including investors. Rachel cost herself $700,000 because she disrespected the views of those who were not in total agreement. We will never know what could have happened to her business because she chooses to fight rather than understand opposing views and use it as a platform for discussion rather than divisiveness.

How many of us are trying to grow our pipelines, close more accounts, become an industry expert while feeling fulfilled? Many people are self-sabotaging because they forget the principle behind the achievement is to love one another and treat every human with dignity and respect.

As humans, we all want to be part of something larger. We want to believe and feel we have a purpose. Once someone forms an identity, it affects how they perceive others with similar or divergent views. We like people that agree with us and feel less connected to those that don't. If you want to sell to everyone, stay out of that game. Don't give people a reason to resent you before they even meet you.

How many of your clients or prospects are you connected to on social media? Are your accounts private? Do you know how to disagree with someone and still have respect for their views? Do you know how to have a differing opinion and stay cordial?

COACH KLYN'S HOMEWORK TO DO BEFORE DAY 21:

1. Map out your online and social media presence.

   _____

   _____

   _____

   _____

2. Google yourself. What did you discover? Did anything surprise you?

   _____

   _____

   _____

   _____

3. If you have anything on social media or online that could cost you opportunities, delete it.

DAY 21:
Gratitude

"You can have everything in life you want, if you will just help enough other people get what they want."

– Zig Ziglar

We often forget how important it is to be grateful. If you aren't thankful for one customer, you don't deserve two. Gratitude is the great equalizer in life.

As the co-founder of a company called Happyest, we teach employees how to start a gratitude challenge in their own lives to activate the part of the brain that helps them see the positivity around them. Far too often in sales, we get so bogged down with problems and rejection that we forget to look up from our computers and experience what's great.

Gratitude improves health and wellness, incites feelings of relaxation and calm, and fires off neurons that help us manage all life events. In one famous study from the University of Pennsylvania, psychologists asked participants to write a letter of gratitude to someone they feel was never adequately thanked, once a week. The participants immediately exhibited a huge increase in personal happiness scores against a control group. In fact, their happiness improved more than any other form of intervention the psychologists tried and lasted for over a month.

A beautiful soul in the fitness industry called me this summer in tears claiming she didn't have a purpose in her career and hated life. I asked her to put her hand on her heart, close her eyes, breathe in through her nose for a count of 5, and exhale for 6 seconds. I encouraged her to think about all the people she is grateful for. I asked her to see those faces in her mind and feel that love in her heart.

She started to cry.

After bringing her out of the meditation, I instructed her to create a list of 50 life events she was grateful for experiencing. When finished with that list, she could then make a career decision based on her purpose.

Be grateful now for the customers you do have.

Be grateful now for the career you have.

Be grateful for those in your life who have shaped what made you who you are today.

Be grateful someone loves you enough to give you feedback on how to improve.

Be grateful you are breathing air right now.

COACH KLYN'S HOMEWORK TO DO BEFORE DAY 22:

1. Put your hand on your heart. Close your eyes. Breathe in through your nose for a count of 5 and exhale for a count of 6.

2. Allow your mind to see the faces and feel the love of those you who have made a difference in your life.

3. Write 50 things you are grateful for now.

_____

_____

_____

_____

_____

_____

_____

_____

_____

_____

_____

_____

_____

DAY 22:
Balance

"Great salespeople are relationship builders who provide value and help their customers win."

– Jeffrey Gitomer

I don't care how much this book has helped you improve your career productivity and profitability if you failed to spend quality time with those you love.

It's a hard lesson to understand.

If you're like me, your calendar is continuously full. When was the last time you booked something you genuinely enjoyed on your calendar and treated it as a priority?

Most people forget to connect with those who live with them. I've been guilty. Far too often, I wake up and rush to my office, failing to look at my fiance and wish him well before a long day at work. Far too often, my fiance comes home and runs to the couch where our 3-pound dog, Chanel, jumps up on him and licks his face. Sometimes I feel a little abandoned. Why does he care more about our dog than seeing me? It's simple. The dog lets him know how important he is. Chanel doesn't care if he's ten minutes late for dinner or forgot to pick up wine. She's just happy to see him.

Far too often, we forget how to treat those we love the most because we are busy thinking about how we want them to treat us. We say, "I love you," quickly and hastily. We rush out the door with a beeping phone and forget to connect with the people in our homes.

Remember what made you love the people in your network and take some time today to reach out to them individually and explain what a difference they've made in your life. When I first came up with this philosophy, people thought I lost my mind. "But Klyn, how can we make time for this?" they'd ask.

I don't care if you have to schedule "love" calls for Tuesday at 2 pm to replace your Starbucks run. Design your calendar to include weekly time to express love and gratitude to those who have helped you along the way. I created a list of those who have impacted my life and make it a point to reach out to them. As a result, when I have news to share or something I need help with, my network has my back. Do your peers have your back? If your answer is no, recognize it may be because you haven't had theirs.

COACH KLYN'S HOMEWORK TO DO BEFORE DAY 23:

1. Make a list of everyone you want to express love and appreciation for.

   _____

   _____

   _____

   _____

2. Schedule time every month to have a conversation with them. Write down the schedule if you need to.

   _____

   _____

3. Think of three people that you care for but lost connection with. Reach out to them and say hi.

   _____

   _____

   _____

DAY 23:
Fishing with Bubblegum

"Pretend that every single person you meet has a sign around his or her neck that says, 'Make me feel important.' Not only will you succeed in sales, you will succeed in life."

– Mary Kay Ash

C hances are your sales have exploded or are well on their way since you started this 30-day challenge. Time to check in: have you been actively listening to your calls?

If you aren't listening to yourself, you aren't growing. The first time I went back and watched my keynotes, I cringed. They were horrible! I watched, I listened, and I pivoted. Remember the power of the pivot we talked about earlier?

Have you ever noticed that when people talk to you, they tend to break off eye contact? This happens because looking at someone in the eyes takes more mental power than looking away. The combined effort of reading someone's eyes, thinking about your next word, and forming speech creates a brain overload and POOF. We look away. Our brainpower is limited.

You can see the same effect when someone turns down the radio when they get lost. The combination of loud noises, driving, and thinking about where you need to go can be overwhelming.

You might think that you are able to analyze your sales performances on your own. But the truth is that it's too much effort for most of us to do all at once. Record yourself working. If you are unable to close a deal, work backward on the steps you've outlined in your company's playbook to see where your shortcomings are. When you know what part of the sales process you struggle with, you can triage it and prevent that mistake from happening again. Ask your manager or top producer in your firm to coach you through the error.

Frequently, we get the sale and we carry on our merry little way to write up the order and forget that sometimes even a blind squirrel finds an acorn.

True story: my mom, dad, brother, and I were on a fishing trip in Canada while I was in high school. My brother, a junior, wanted to get off the boat and hang out with the other high-school kids. Annoyed we were still fishing after 3 hours; he took bubble gum out of his mouth and put it on the end of a hook. My brother caught a northern Pike with chewed bubble gum!

Are your sales high because you are good at what you do or because your industry is growing right now and it's relatively easy? Do your sales come from skill or luck? Are you listening to yourself and checking your results against your process? Do you build rapport throughout the entire call instead of a 2-3 canned sentence in the beginning?

Regardless of industry, you should be getting referrals. If most of your business comes from inbound marketing or leads outside of your job duty - you have room for growth.

COACH KLYN'S HOMEWORK TO DO BEFORE DAY 24:

1. Evaluate yourself against your industry. How much of your success is due to the product and market conditions vs. your actual skill?

_____

_____

_____

_____

2. Listen attentively to your calls, and when you have a moment, you find yourself cringing. Analyze and improve.

_____

_____

_____

_____

DAY 24:
Management

"I don't like that man. I must get to know him better."

– Abraham Lincoln

There are incompetent managers, just like there are incompetent salespeople. Now I am not saying your manager isn't great, but I want to be clear, you are the CEO of your career. If you are waiting for your manager to review your calls and give feedback, you're on your way to the bottom tier of professionals.

The Harvard Business Review once asked 3,875 people who'd received negative feedback from their manager if they were surprised or already aware of the raised problem. An astonishing 74% of them already knew and were expecting the critique. We place too much emphasis on what others think instead of looking inwards. More likely than not, you already know what needs to be done.

High achievers don't wait for the manager to tell them how to improve. They are personally accountable for their results and progress. They go to their manager for improvement questions, but they don't exclusively rely on that feedback.

You have to know when you are mediocre. You have to know when you are great. And you can't wait for others to tell you. Find that fire inside you, your internal compass, and trust it. Curse yourself out when you have a terrible day and become your own cheerleader.

Never wait on your manager for feedback. Get proactive. Do not wait for your scheduled managerial review to hear how they feel about your performance. The top salespeople study to improve and have a detailed plan on how they won't make the same mistake twice.

COACH KLYN'S HOMEWORK TO DO BEFORE DAY 25:

1. If you were in your manager's shoes right now, what three things (or more) would you tell yourself to improve?

   i._____

   ii._____

   iii._____

2. Which of these is your top priority and how can you start improving it tomorrow?

   _____

   _____

   _____

   _____

DAY 25:
Urgency

"The earlier you make decisions; the more time those decisions have to turn into measurable results"

- Klyn Elsbury in *I AM __ The Untold Story of Success*

A sense of urgency is the key to success - everything now, nothing later.

When I was born, my family was instructed to plan my funeral. They were told again to plan a funeral when I slipped into ketoacidosis, a diabetic coma when I was a teenager. In my early twenties, my lung function hit 30%, and again, told to plan that funeral. When I filed for social security disability, I had spent over 150 days in the hospital that year. My time was up.

I'm in my thirties now, and chances are, I'm healthier than most of the salespeople reading this. It's a strong sense of urgency. And I want you to know your life is ending as you read this.

Yes, you will die. Stop putting things off for someday. Someday never comes. Bonnie Ware is an Australian nurse, counselor, and author who spent years working in palliative care - taking care of people in the last stages of their life. In her 2012 book, she chronicles that the number 1 regret people had before dying, which was "I wish I'd had the courage to live a life true to myself, not the life others expected of me." Don't let this be you. Figure out what you want in your life and career, then pursue it.

For sales managers who hire, try this fun experiment to see how much of a sense of urgency a representative has. Give the candidate an assignment (some of my favorites include listening to previous employees' calls or creating a presentation on overcoming objections). If they respond within 24 hours, you can feel reasonably assured they will respond to your customers in 24 hours. If they take a week, you may not be able to trust they won't take a week to get back with your customers.

How real is it for you that your time is running out? How deep is your sense of urgency?

I want a life for you that is full of unimaginable prosperity, and you wouldn't be reading this if you didn't want that for your life too!

COACH KLYN'S HOMEWORK TO DO BEFORE DAY 26:

1. Look at your bucket list and schedule one thing to do in the next 13 weeks. No excuses.

   _____

   _____

2. Analyze how long it takes you to get back with someone. Are you acting with a sense of urgency?

   _____

   _____

DAY 26:
Stepping Stones

"I am who I am today because of the choices I made yesterday."

– Eleanor Roosevelt

I t takes one person in a company to destroy the years of work that went into building it. We have all met a toxic teammate. When one employee becomes negative and only does the minimum at their job, it creates a tone for the organization's rest.

In 2015, Cornerstone OnDemand created a report titled *"Toxic Employees in the Workplace"* detailing the effects a toxic coworker can have on an organization. First, they accumulated a dataset of approximately 63,000 hired employees spanning 250,000 observations. They identified toxic employees, which they defined as those who were terminated for "toxic behavior" such as misconduct, workplace violence, sexual harassment, fraud, or other violations of company policy. They found that good employees who were forced to work with toxic employees quit at a 54% higher rate.

Even more concerning, their research also found that toxic behavior is contagious. Toxic employees were more likely to occur in larger teams. Likewise, employees were more likely to engage in toxic behavior if they were exposed to other toxic employees.

When a high achiever starts to wane in performance, address it proactively. If they start taking too much time off, develop a cynical attitude, and only do the minimum required, it may be time to check-in. I've discovered a genuine conversation with someone who is struggling can improve the morale of the team. Chances are you can save their career and the company. If they need time to get back to where they were, honor it and encourage it.

Now and then toxicity can creep into an organization. When one employee becomes "cancerous," the rest of the organization will follow. Second and third-tier quadrants of salespeople start to follow suit, and management is left scratching their heads on how to fix it. The truth is, aside from getting rid of cancer, there isn't a lot left to do.

For the employees reading this, if you notice your organization is starting to accept mediocrity and you've built your expertise and pipeline, leave. If you have cancer, recognize that the attitude of "just getting by" is the first to go when times get challenging.

If you're going through a tough time personally, own it with your manager. If they can't accept you need support right now, find another manager. I know hundreds of progressive companies who care about their employees. If you're a high achiever, I'll create an introduction for you.

COACH KLYN'S HOMEWORK TO DO BEFORE DAY 27:

1. Can you identify one or more cancerous employees on your team? If so, what can you do to insulate yourself from their behavior?

_____

_____

_____

_____

2. Are you doing the bare minimum? Are you riding on the coattails of the experts?

_____

_____

3. If you are, level up. Ask your manager to give you a 360-degree review and provide you with actionable critiques.

_____

_____

_____

_____

DAY 27:
Proactive Pipelining

"Our greatest weakness lies in giving up. The most certain way to succeed is to try just one more time."

– Thomas Edison

Forecasting has a love/hate relationship with most representatives. We want to be modest in our models because we can justify our egos if we are above quota. If we forecast low and close slightly above that, we look skilled.

Recognize, that kind of guesswork is a losing mentality.

Set goals that freak you out a little bit. Set goals that give you butterflies when you discuss them with others. Believe it or not, those butterflies are actually good for you. In their 2008 study, *"Increasing well-being through teaching goal-setting and planning skills"*, MacLeod, Coates & Hetherton from the University of London found that goal setting did more than just help people be more productive. They discovered that goal setting actually increased their subject's well-being.

I know you may be seeking the psychological benefit of setting a lower goal, so you feel better about yourself when you reach it. Yet, I've never known another person who I genuinely admired that had that approach. Think about the person who has the success you want. How do you think they set their goals?

A representative I was coaching in 2019 had the goal of closing $50 million in international accounts. The company average was $15 million per territory account executive. It was an aggressive goal. Together the two of us created a plan. He worked on the plan. That year, he did not achieve his goal. He ended the year with $47 million in new account sales.

What do you think their manager did?

Shockingly, they were upset that the representative was wrongly forecasted! To understand what went wrong with the forecast, the manager began excessive tracking of the representative's activity in the CRM. They required more reports, reporting, and meetings. Rather than focus on what the representative did correctly to gain a top spot in the company, they tracked a CRM. It's a great example of when management doesn't deserve the achievement on their team. And he quit. I explained to him that he is not a tree. He can move, and he did.

Our $47 million a year producer now works for the competitor. When you set big goals, you instantly become more attractive to the marketplace and have more power over the choices you can make. If you're a top performer, don't allow a CRM to slow you down. Hire an assistant (or convince your manager to hire you one) to take care of the paperwork, so you can focus on what you do best, which should be selling.

COACH KLYN'S HOMEWORK TO DO BEFORE DAY 28:

1. What's your forecasted goal? Quota?

   _____

   _____

2. Great, now add 10-20% to your personal goal. What's the new number?

   _____

   _____

3. Great, now execute on it.

4. Get an assistant if you need to. Get out of paperwork nightmares and back into the closing.,

5. Tweet me proof, @KlynElsbury the #30thoughts

DAY 28:
Curiosity

"Most of the important things in the world have been accomplished by people who have kept on trying when there seemed to be no hope at all."

– Dale Carnegie

Think back to when you first started your current job. Do you remember that call you got from the hiring manager telling you that you got the job? You probably pumped your fists, let out a good cheer, and told your friends, family, and loved ones. What goals and aspirations did you have? Do you still have them, or have they faded into a routine?

The tricky thing about our society is we think it's okay to tell everyone about our goals. Our brains go into overdrive. We share how great we plan to be and start working on that plan. We forget about the chapter on momentum. Time passes, and we realize nobody follows up with our ambitious visions. We aren't held accountable, so we abandon our ambitions in hopes of finding something else to cling to long enough to feel important.

Is your band-aid ripped off yet?

Make your change your reality. The words you speak don't describe the world. They create it. Yes, you read that correctly. Your words create your world. Champions are built, not born. Look at your pipeline and take the time today to reach out to your favorite customers. Call them up, ask how they are doing, start to work on the referrals. Remember, you can have big goals, but you also need to have a big heart.

Sales are the transfer of trust. The know, like, and trust factor makes high achievers out of regular joes. Curiosity is the hack to never getting bored with your product, customers, and industry.

What do you know about your best customers? Are you following them and encouraging their life journey online? Do you know what their dreams are or what makes them truly happy?

Enjoy the process of getting curious about your best customers and using that curiosity to create the next conversation.

COACH KLYN'S HOMEWORK TO DO BEFORE DAY 29:

1. What questions can you ask your best customers?

_____

_____

_____

_____

2. How can you stay curious about them, their struggles, their accomplishments, and their goals?

_____

_____

_____

_____

3. Google the best questions to ask your friends and family - tons of books will pop up. Order one and memorize 15-20 of these questions. Try it out the next time a group of people comes together.

DAY 29:
You Don't Get What You Deserve

"I have never worked a day in my life without selling. If I believe in something, I sell it, and I sell it hard."

-Estée Lauder

W hen I was a kid, I would read my dad's selling magazines. Don't ask why. I was a weird kid. One day as I flipped through the pages, I remembered seeing a giant ad on one of the sections paid for by a sales trainer. The photo was of a fortune cookie. The quote was simple: "In life, you don't get what you deserve, you get what you negotiate for."

The reason so many sales reps don't become top producers isn't because they aren't skilled. They know the product, features, and benefits better than anyone else in the company, yet their sales are lackluster. It's easy to comfort yourself in busy work and memorize features rather than take on the challenge of asking for a sale.

You see, the rejection that comes with asking for the sale is too painful for most people to take, so they delay it. From that delay there's other consequences like having lower sales, embarrassment, and eventually finding another career.

Humans are hard-wired to avoid social rejection. For our ancestors, being cut out from a tribe would mean certain death. Social rejection is so dangerous that it can be physically painful. In fact, researchers have found that Acetaminophen, the active ingredient in Tylenol, can actually help alleviate the pain of social disappointment in much the same way it does for chronic pain (not that I'm encouraging you to pop Tylenol when you make your calls).

Fear of that social rejection, and the pain that comes with it, can hold you back. However, there is a way around it. When you are asking for business, create a conversation instead of giving a pitch. This allows you to flush out the real objections the buyer has. Many salespeople believe that when a customer responds with hesitation or objections, they aren't interested in the product. This is not true. When a customer asks you a question, it isn't an objection. It's a buying signal they want to learn more.

How many times in your life do you ask someone a question and want them to help you find a solution? That's all the buyers are doing, asking you to make a solution clearer for them. We hate to be told what to do. We love to figure out the solution with an expert.

The question then becomes, why are so many salespeople afraid to ask for the business?

And remember, you don't get what you deserve. You get what you can negotiate.

COACH KLYN'S HOMEWORK TO DO BEFORE DAY 30:

1. Analyze yourself. How much do you let the fear of rejection dictate your sales?

_____

_____

2. How often do you feel nervous or anxious while on a call or pitch?

_____

_____

3. If either of those is high, what can you do to bring them down? (HINT: Go back and reread the chapter on how to "can" your plan.)

_____

_____

_____

_____

DAY 30:
Love Yourself

"Sales are contingent upon the attitude of the salesman – not the attitude of the prospect."

– W. Clement Stone

I've been hard on you for 30 days. When I first started consulting, I got the label of being "too tough." Interestingly, the employees who thought I was too strict didn't want to make the changes in their lives to explode their sales and improve the overall quality of their lives.

They made excuses.

They lived their excuses.

They had a mediocre mind, and anyone who countered those belief systems became the enemy.

They all quit a career in sales.

The type of person who goes out and buys a book like this, follows the coaching questions, and commits to a higher quality of life, will have a higher quality of life. And it takes one heck of a person to take such harsh feedback and realities and learn to love themselves in the process.

Companies improve when mediocrity isn't tolerated.

My friends, sales is the most beautiful and rewarding profession there is. You focus on growth, feedback, and action. You get rejected daily, you focus on improvement, opportunities happen, and you become a winner. Then after 30 days, the numbers reset, and you're back to only being as good as the prior month.

Love who you are. Embrace your struggles and what they teach you. Be generous with yourself. Be grateful for the people in your life. Be thankful for those customers who don't buy, for they taught you something. Be thankful for those raving fans who send referrals. Be grateful for that manager who takes the time to help you. Be thankful you've learned how to help yourself. Be thankful for the person who recommended that you read this book. Be thankful for the part of your brain that encouraged you to keep reading and continue implementing what you've learned. Be grateful for all you've overcome and all that's next for you in your journey.

Champions are built, not born.

Klyn Elsbury

www.missklyn.com

Stay connected; stay motivated.

Get more from Klyn Elsbury.

I t's time to step into the life of exceeding quotas, balancing family, and taking care of yourself! Featuring inspirational messages from Klyn, a happy, healthy, motivated mind is one click away with the free podcast (steaming everywhere) and her weekly email series.

Visit www.missklyn.com to sign up today.

About your sales coach, Klyn Elsbury:

B orn with cystic fibrosis, Klyn has endured over 67 hospitalizations and grew up inside the walls of a hospital isolation ward. To occupy her time and mind, she asked herself, *"why can some people accomplish incredible feats even when it seems as if their world is falling apart?"*

She leveraged the information she uncovered in hospital walls and applied it to her recruiting career in her 20's, where she won multiple awards. In 2015, her health plummeted, and she started spending upwards of 6 months a year in the hospital.

After losing her recruiting career, Klyn decided to write her first book, *I AM   The Untold Story Of Success*. Using Linkedin between treatments, she got national news coverage regarding pharmaceutical pricing gouging. She and her book skyrocketed to becoming an international bestseller, allowing her to get off social security services.

She launched her online course, <u>Shark School</u>, teaching social media selling tactics for explosive growth in today's virtual world. And in 2018, she created a sales certification program teaching corporations how to optimize their sales processes by creating custom sales playbooks and systems proven to improve closing ratios, raise customer satisfaction, and create lasting employee motivation.

Klyn's podcast (The Truth About Sales), online courses, corporate training, and keynotes motivate and teach high-performance tactics for an estimated 200,000 minds a month. One of the leading experts blending motivation and inspiration using neuroscience for corporate America, Klyn's audiences are growth-oriented businesses and associations looking to improve their competitive edge.

In 2019, just two years after getting off of social security, she hit six figures, and through strategic partnerships in 2020 she created her first 7 figure deal, proving to the world that it doesn't matter what your genetic code says,

"Champions are built, not born."

CPSIA information can be obtained
at www.ICGtesting.com
Printed in the USA
LVHW052127040321
680608LV00015B/2567